YOUR CV:

Would you put a stamp on it?

PLAN YOUR CAREER MOVE WITH PURPOSE

DENISE MATTHEWS

WOULD YOU PUT A STAMP ON IT?

Congratulations on taking a step towards consciously planning your career change. As a specialist recruiter, I am often surprised at how little planning most candidates put into their job change strategy, instead of using the fastest finger first technique!

When I first became a recruiter the process to apply for a role was so detailed (and arduous!) – read the newspaper vacancy sections, decide on your CV format, type(!!) your CV and write a covering letter, find the right envelope, add your stamp, and walk to a red post-box. This process took effort and investment of your time, so as recruiters we tended to receive a much higher standard, (if less volume), of applications. The arrival of online job sites and the option to have a CV stored ready to send at any time has made it easy to hit 'apply' and see what happens. Consequently, recruiters are deluged with applications, making it almost impossible to give quality feedback to the unsuccessful as they instead focus on working with the candidates who stand out to get their clients the best possible result.

This journal is designed with the goal of you making yourself a project. It is not a non-fiction specialist careers management book. There are lots of great versions of these;. This journal is all about stimulating new or reinvigorating old ideas and managing your applications mindfully, use it alongside some of the excellent careers' books available, some of which I have referenced in here.

Good luck!

Denise

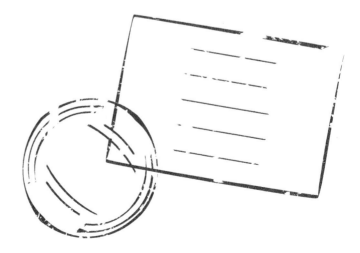

ABOUT DENISE MATTHEWS

Denise Matthews has a wealth of experience in retail, recruitment and as a licensed career coach with so many people wanting or needing to make a career change since the pandemic, Denise ensures that they go on to find roles they love and that really light them up! It's what she's enjoyed for most of her career, so she wants to help others experience the same job satisfaction.

Following a successful senior retail career, Denise joined a retail-focused recruitment agency in central London learning all about recruitment and this ultimately inspired her to set up her own business with a former colleague. That's when The One Consultancy was born. Here as an executive head-hunter, Denise also trained as an ILM qualified Coach, to be able to help her candidates fulfil their true potential in their new positions. Denise then worked for some market-leading recruitment organisations, developing her skills and knowledge before moving client-side to join ASOS where she and her team helped to grow the contact centre to meet the needs of their fantastic international business growth. Denise decided to enhance her skills with an additional qualification in Career Coaching and launched Elevate Careers Coaching.

It's provided a real lifeline to employees throughout lockdown, who were looking for not only their next career move but a role that they really love!

As well as being ILM level 7 qualified as a Coach, Denise is also a licensed career coach through the Firework Network, which is an advanced career change coaching programme, and one of the most well-respected, credible training programmes of its type, with a 17-year track record.

Find out more about working with Denise on her career change programmes:

'Re-Start; Your Personal Career Coaching Programme'
'Project You, mindful career planning'

Clarity, Discovery, and Action on the Elevate Careers website:

elevatecareerscoach.com

And follow her on Instagram and Facebook for helpful advice and tips on managing your job search:

- elevate_careerscoaching
- elevatecareerscoaching
- denisematthews

PROJECT YOU

How to use your journal

At work when we are asked to review a process or design a new idea, we take a considered approach. Mapping the journey, consulting with colleagues, team meetings looking at the rationale, timelines, cost, obstacles, knowledge gaps, expert advice so you know from pressing go on the project that you have a goal, a timeline, and some ideas about addressing challenges along the way. However, candidates often approach their career change with more of a scattergun approach. Looking on job sites at the weekend, a hasty update of their CV and no real end goal in mind other than 'I need a change' or 'I want more money'! Take the time now to really think about your career plans – think more than one job ahead as you'll need a roadmap to get to your destination, think about the timing as well as the skills.

To achieve this will take time as you work through the exercises in this journal. The exercises originate from carefully tailored research into best practices in career evaluation and transition, it's backed up by my own experience as a personal development and career coach.

The journal aims to help you take a journey from uncertainty about your present career and not knowing what your next step might be, through to having a clear vision of a career that is absolutely right for you. Having a plan for how to create your plan and by keeping records in the Action section of your activity and outcomes, you will learn more about yourself and identify patterns. This will help to improve your applications and interview performance and perhaps even completely change your strategy. It is a journey of discovery both for now and in the future. I anticipate this journal will bring out skills and thoughts which will be useful long term, so keep it and keep adding to the pages in anticipation of the next time you are once again ready for a move!

CLARITY

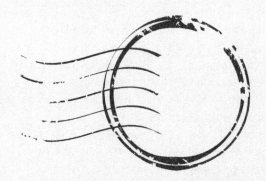

Clarity about
what matters,
provides clarity
about what does not.

CAL NEWPORT

FINDING CLARITY – WHY IT'S IMPORTANT

- Do you have the Sunday evening 'dread feeling' about going into work the next day?

- Do you have a what is considered by others to be a good career, but you feel sure there are better options which will take away the feelings of being frustrated and unfulfilled?

- Are you looking for a career shift or swap?

- Has your job search so far resulted in disappointment and rejection or negative recruiter feedback – leaving you feeling panicked that nothing will work?

If you have purchased this journal, you have most likely gone through many of these emotions and now it's 'decision made'. You are going to make a move or switch but maybe you're still not yet clear what that may actually mean.

In my experience of coaching career changers, 'Clarity' comes from identifying the outcome you want, discovering what opportunities there are and then taking positive action. This journal will help you with planning your career search and reflecting on your learnings along the way, so that the role you eventually accept is a good fit for your aspirations.

As part of your journey towards your career switch or move, you may need to invest time and energy finding out about other sectors and careers, perhaps spending (unpaid) time, with people to fill your knowledge gaps or invest time on research.

"Remember if you don't invest why should people or companies invest in you?"

As I mentioned in the introduction, the 'fastest finger first' approach often means not all the roles you apply for are relevant, so they end in multiple rejections, and this cycle inevitably creates a lack of confidence in yourself. By applying for the 'right' opportunities and concentrating on the results you achieve, the chances of a successful outcome are greatly improved.
I see a visible change in people when they decide the time is right and have made the decision to change careers, it is one of those decisions often procrastinated about, sometimes leaving it so long that it becomes 'too late'!

It is also possible that you may be approached by a contact or head-hunter, can come as a total surprise. You may not be prepared with the right questions to ask – or even able to think on the spot if it is something you want to discuss further or if it's a straight no thank you. One thing that can happen after an unexpected approach is that it may unsettle you, as it opens possibilities that you may not have considered. This sometimes leads to deciding to explore a move as you will have been shown something potentially more rewarding or exciting.

.................So, having made your decision to switch or change, what next?

A useful exercise can be to complete an online career aptitude test to help you with insights into which career is likely to be a good fit for your personality. Whilst not all of these tests are scientifically validated, they can be helpful in opening up new ideas for you to explore - an open mind is a vital part of this process for change.

FREE CAREER APTITUDE TESTS

The following tests are available for free online and it is worthwhile spending some time exploring the outcomes of your results:

- **123 Career Test:** This is a popular aptitude test which helps you gain insight into the careers that best fit your personality. It will also help you learn what kind of working environments and occupations may suit you.

- **Human Metrics:** Using both Jung's Typology and Myers-Briggs insights, Human Metrics takes you through 64 questions to rate you on both scales. The results explain to you how each piece relates to your personality type.

- **Red Bull Wingfinder:** Take a free 35-minute online personality assessment to identify and leverage your strengths in four different areas of your personality, including; connections, creativity, thinking, and drive. Wingfinder test takers immediately receive a free 19-page feedback report containing an analysis of their strengths, along with advice, and coaching from Red Bull athletes who have the same strengths.

Looking at your plans to make a career change is like planning a journey where the roadmap has wide lanes with lots of options! These lanes can be looked at in the following way□

EASY STREET

This is when you decide to take the natural next step from your current job. This may be more responsibility, larger budget, team accountability, or a sideways move to learn more about a different area of your function. These are natural first steps to consider and will be one of the easiest to follow through on.

FLIPPING

Perhaps you have identified that you would like to utilise your existing skills in a different way or function - or even switch to a completely new industry. Use the exercises in your journal to think about your skills and ideas on how you could pivot to a different area or company/sector.

AMBITION

How often have you watched someone more senior and thought you could do their role more effectively? And then convinced yourself it's not a feasible idea? Maybe with self-doubt stopping you from putting yourself forward when the opportunities arise or even asking the right questions to support your own development and knowledge, so that you are ready. Work out what creates that feeling of negativity and seek support to fill any skills gaps you identify then develop an action plan with clear timelines and goals.

DREAMING

Imagining possibilities for a change in your career is a great place to start 'Project You'. Take away all the barriers that you may have created over the years and open your mind to ideas which are built on your natural interests and existing or aspirational skills. To gain clarity about your career planning one of my favourite tools as a Firework Careers Coach, is an exercise designed by John Lees called:

"If all jobs paid the same.... what would I do for a living?"

Take some time to reflect on this thought provoking question and use the next page to record your notes and thoughts on the diagram.

IF ALL JOBS PAID THE SAME...
what would I do for a living?

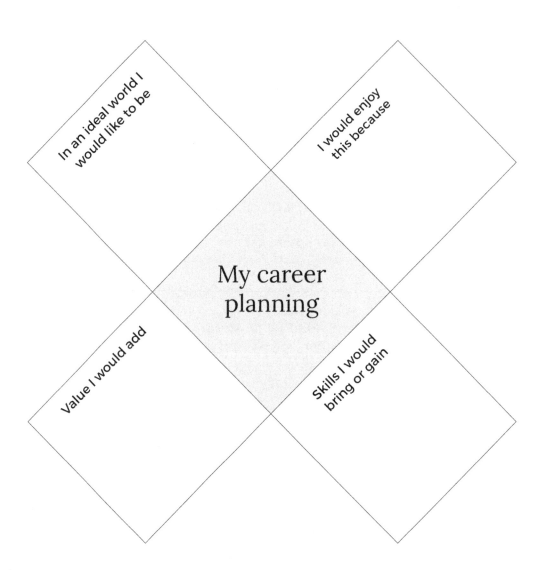

In an ideal world I would like to be

I would enjoy this because

My career planning

Value I would add

Skills I would bring or gain

Review: 'IF ALL JOBS PAID THE SAME'

- How did you feel when faced with the first question?

- Have you ever thought before about what you may do in your career if there were no limits?

- Did it feel like you could just use your imagination and dig deep for some exciting ideas or did the '**yes but**' factor stop you from dreaming?

An important part of making a positive move forward, and for the right reasons, is to really understand yourself. All of these exercises are helping you to acknowledge what is important to you. Taking that into account and looking back on the diagram, write down without over-thinking it, as many answers as you can to the 4 questions. Remember there are no limits to what you can think about whilst doing this - mechanic, CEO, trapeze artist, journalist - be as open minded as you possibly can!

_____

_____

_____

_____

_____

_____

_____

_____

_____

_____

_____

_____

_____

_____

_____

'IF ALL JOBS PAID THE SAME I WOULD......'

'IF ALL JOBS PAID THE SAME I WOULD......'

Having looked at the four possible options, the next thing to do is identify 'what' you need to know and 'who' can help you.

The comment from others, which stops most job changers making a move is... 'be realistic'. So be prepared for this from family & friends as it can stop you in your tracks. Whilst you are motivated and aspiring to find a job you really love, there will be internal pressure from yourself, and inevitably those around you, to find a nice safe job which is 'OK' and 'pays the bills'.

Some people I meet are in jobs they 'fell into', often because of school careers advice, or uncertainty around their future opportunities. Some of you will have chosen a profession because your parents encouraged you to follow a safe 'professional route'. However, you have never settled into a happy place in your career or found a job you love.

TRANSFERABLE SKILLS

If using the 'If all jobs paid the same' exercise inspired you to think about your dream job/s – then take your research much deeper. Investigate the content of these roles as there will most likely be elements of them which you can identify in 'available job opportunities', meaning it would not be a total re-training exercise.

Also identifying that you have transferable skills keeps your job search energy high and gives you the motivation to keep applying - even when the going gets tough, as you recognise you have the skills and attributes to be successful in a job you love.

You may not be looking for a complete career switch but are tired of, or bored, with your current role; perhaps there are opportunities in your current company which could be a great fit? Talk to your line Manager or HR about how they view your skills and find out the possibilities for internal moves and what you would need to do to be considered. All of this should also clarify if you are looking for a change of career or a change of workplace – there is a significant difference, so don't leap until you are sure.

I often meet people at this point, as working with a careers coach can give you tools and support to identify clarity on your next steps which is a key part of 'Project You'. If you have a good line manager or work mentor, talk to them and this is also a great opportunity to seek support from your wider network.

HOW DO I GET EXPERIENCE IN A NEW FIELD?

You are probably anxious about getting experience in a new field. You can consider:

- **Online education:** You can learn skills on your own device, in your own time, and get a certificate or degree that can help boost your skills & CV, and make your application more attractive to potential employers.

- **Start a side hustle:** You could start an entry-level side job in the new career field you're pursuing, so you can learn the ropes under someone else and gain experience. Or, you could explore volunteer/adult internship opportunities that provide you with experience.

- **Work with a career coach:** If you want to switch careers, a career coach can help you find connections, guide you in the right direction of what to learn and provide you with recommendations for skills to study, before you embark on a job search. Working with a career coach is an investment, but it may pay off by helping you to find a more fulfilling career.

Done well, career change is a time-consuming project but remember that 'Project YOU' has clear goals and targets and as with any project you will need to prioritise your actions and plans. By consciously planning the steps and actions for your career change, you will find that the law of attraction will mean you naturally identify opportunities for further discovery - which could be new book titles to read, networking events to attend, societies to join or challenges and courses to sign up to.

DISCOVERY

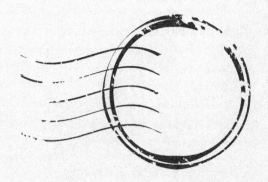

Don't judge
the day by the
harvest you reap
but the seeds
that you plant.

ROBERT LOUIS STEVENSON

NO LIMITS - DREAM OF POSSIBILITIES!

Whilst you have spent some time establishing clarity, (along with perhaps some dreaming!), about what you are looking for in the next stage of your career, you should have started to think about how to make your plans a reality. As you spend time exploring your ideas do not allow your thoughts to be restrictive – to make the best of the work you have already done you must not be held back by considerations of what is possible at this stage. Your future career vision is currently in your plans – now you need to work out 'how' you can enjoy success.

Steve Jobs, founder of Apple said, "Your time is limited, so don't waste it living someone else's life. Don't be trapped by dogma - which is living with the results of other people's thinking. Don't let the noise of other's opinions drown out your own inner voice. And most important, have the courage to follow your heart and intuition. They somehow already know what you truly want to become. Everything else is secondary.".

The Discovery section is about you taking action to explore the options you have identified in more detail, This is a vital part of your career change journey, so rather than just looking at options on the surface, dig deep into why you have created your list of jobs to explore. Think about why you wrote it down, what exactly appeals to you, if you were this ....., what would be great about it? What is the underlying attraction to that role? Be creative in your ideas and really understand why they appeal to you. Then when applying for those roles you really can articulate why, whilst starting to look at reality and possibilities for your search/change.

YOUR CURRENT REALITY

Write down below all the aspects of your current reality in relation to your future career vision. Include all your strengths, abilities, qualities, skills, training and qualifications. Consider how these match your future aspirations as well as including your values, financial situation and family information. Your list should include both the positive and negatives to give you an overall picture so that you can identify any knowledge and skill gaps. This may highlight the need for you to do further training or qualifications and this may be something you can do whilst in your current role. If you identify that you need stronger networking connections or need to join professional organisations, then you need to make a plan of what and how you will do this.

REALITY CHECK

On the opposite page I have included a reality check exercise, and in the tracking section of your journal you will find one of these for every role you apply for - this is part of your conscious approach to your application. Remember, done correctly and responsibly applying for a role is a time consuming job in itself, so invest your time and energy into applying for the right opportunity. The reality checker is a crucial part of this process. As you can see from the scores on the example page, the percentage match to the role is c.70%. This means that this a role worth applying for, as whilst you may not have the level of experience sought in some areas, you are well qualified in others. Harsh reality is that less than a 50% match will almost always result in a rejection, but 70% and above will be a strong application.

The key benefit of this exercise is that you have completed a deep dive into what the recruiter is looking for and matched it to your own experience, so if called for an interview you will be prepared with good evidential responses to the interviewer's questions.

Good interview preparation is essential for every role - easy to say, and most people see this as a Google search to find out facts about the company. Whereas, in reality a recruiter will be looking for the 'why' you have applied and 'how' you fit the role. In brief, so the knowledge of how many cities they trade in or their last year revenue, will fade into insignificance if you have not done your personal planning and research.

(NB: Blank forms to complete this exercise are included in the Application Tracker section of your journal.)

In the tracker section of the journal, you will see a blank template of the below form included, which you should use for every role you apply for.

This example gives you an idea of how to use it.

JOB TITLE: Marketing Manager

COMPANY: New Company

From the advert and job description identify knowledge, experience and skills sought:

KNOWLEDGE & SKILLS SOUGHT	MY SKILLS	EXPERIENCE SOUGHT	MY EXPERIENCE
Exceptional communication skills: **Y**	Multi-channel experience: **Y**	CIM qualification: **Studying**	Social media development strategies: **Y**
Liaising with external organisations: **Y**	Co-ordination: **Senior level middle mgt**	Decision maker: **Limited budget mgt 25k**	Sales Fusion 360 software: **N**
High standard of organisational skills: **Y**	Campaign evaluations: **Some exp**	HubSpot Marketing Suite: **Y**	Pharmaceutical industry: **N**
	Creating content internal trends monitoring: **Y**		
	Analytical: **Y**		
	Degree level: **Y**		
	High attention to detail: **Y**		
TOTALS SUMMARY	5 Yes 1 No 3 Limited		5 Yes 1 No 3 Limited

READ, LEARN, RESEARCH

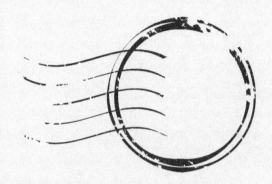

The more you read
The more that you will know
The more that you learn
The more places you'll go!

DR SEUSS

___

In my coaching practice I see clients preparing for change in many ways, which is absolutely right as we all have a different approach to learning and reflection. This guide is designed to give top tips and encourage you to explore more deeply how you can manage this important change and decision. However, reading useful guides about career planning and the type of opportunities other people have enjoyed, or blogs about their journey, can encourage you to take a more considered approach. In turn creating clear goals and identifiing gaps and opportunities.

Whilst it is not always in the job description, the more education, certificates and work experience you have, the better your chances are to be selected above other candidates - it can be the 'stand out factor'. Millennials especially have identified that higher achievements open the door to new opportunities, and educational attainment usually correlates with improved salary potential.

I have listed some books on the next page which I recommend to clients, and suggest that you add to these as you develop your own style in managing your career switch or change.

SUGGESTED READING

Learning by Doing - Professor Graham Gibbs

Gibbs Reflective Cycle

Career Reboot - John Lees

How to get a job you love - John Lees

Switchers - Dawn Graham

What Color is your Parachute? - Richard Bolles with Katharine Brooks

Punch Doubt in the face - Nicolle Merill

The Squiggly Career - Helen Tupper & Sarah Ellis

The Art of Career Change for Introverts - Rebecca Healey

Courageous Career Change - Amy L. Adler

NETWORK...RESEARCH...NETWORK.... NON-STOP!

To be sure that the careers ideas you have are right for you networking and research is vital. To explore your ideas be prepared to invest your own time to gather the information, which will help your decisions about the direction you want to go. I suggest that you talk to your personal contacts, family, friends, coach, HR and mentors, to check out their ideas and advice to gather optimum information. You could join professional organisations to explore more about a specialist topic, or start to read and follow industry journals. Reaching out using your connections to ask if you can shadow professionals is also a great way to gain knowledge and build relationships.

Constantly strive for engagement - think about questions you can ask or comments you can make when following social media posts or talking to people.

Evidence is that about 60% of all jobs are offered without ever being advertised – candidates are sourced through referrals and personal networks. Therefore, it is vital that you build an authentic personal brand so people know what you stand for and will remember to reach out to you when opportunities arise in their network or organisation. You can also attend seminars or conferences related to the areas you are interested in, perhaps get a part time job to get a sense of if it's right for you and to give a better idea of the skills you will need for that role/sector.

BE PREPARED FINANCIALLY

If you are planning a complete career switch you may have to consider that you will need to take a lower paid salary, so prepare for this. A good guide is to reserve the equivalent of a minimum of 6 months living expenses, to provide financial security as you settle into your new career. It is also a good time to speak with a professional financial advisor to get advice on your options. There may be loans, grants or scholarships which can support your transition into the new role, so explore these possibilities.

If you are seeking a more senior role with increased responsibility do some market research on salaries so that you established your expectations.

Use these pages to make notes of the actions you need to explore or take as part of preparation for your change.

ACTION

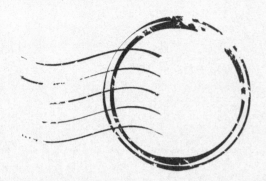

THE secret of getting ahead is getting started.

MARK TWAIN

APPLICATION PLANNING FOR ACTION TAKERS!

Having taken time to think and gain clarity on the type of opportunity you are seeking - this is the all-important section where you will take a deep dive into yourself to identify and acknowledge your strengths and opportunities for development towards your chosen career.

Energy levels and a real commitment to your job search play a major part in how successful you are in finding your career solution. Start by planning your week starting on any day which suits you, (it doesn't have to be Monday!), but it is important that you have used your tracker as your guide to blocking time out for research, meeting contacts or recruiters, networking, follow ups and working on 'yourself'.

It also gives you the space to record every aspect of your search and interview outcomes. This journal is the right size to keep in your bag and jot down notes after interviews or when you have a 'thought' – keep it with you as journalling really does help with clarity for your future plans, both at home and work.

Join my Facebook group '**CAREER planning for ACTION takers**' community for advice and top tips; here you can post questions and share your own experiences in a safe place.

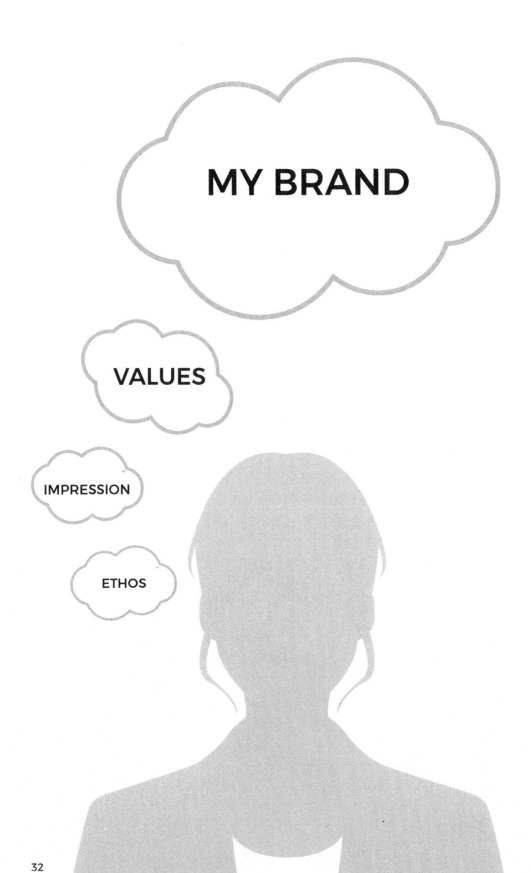

MY BRAND

VALUES

IMPRESSION

ETHOS

YOUR PROFESSIONAL IDENTITY

"All of us need to understand the importance of branding. We are CEOs of our own companies☐ ME Inc. Your most important job is to be head marketeer for the brand called YOU"

TOM PETERS IN FAST COMPANY

Over time the people you work for and with, will subconsciously and consciously identify traits and factors about you. These become their decision makers and essentially create your reputation and consequently 'your brand'.

You may have a reputation as the person who brings in the homemade cakes, always has a paracetamol ready, has a photographic memory, can always get the photocopier going, or the person who likes to work alone and is not really a team player. Be aware and look at yourself from the outside. How do others see you?

Your personal branding should clearly convey to job hirers what you are looking for and what you have to offer.

Write out what you identify with as the elements of your brand on these pages taking into consideration the following points and any you would like to add.

Consider the following factors when thinking about what contributes to your brand:

- Your interactions with others, both written & verbal

- Your body language, tone & volume of voice

- Your social media profiles

- Personal marketing– e.g. LinkedIn, business card, networking

- Associations (teams, friends, groups)

- Hobbies – team or solo

- Environment (cluttered working area, open or closed doors)

- Your actions (speed of response, helpfulness, timekeeping)

- Attitude

- Viewpoints and how you express them

- Your values & how you live them

Your personal branding should clearly convey to job hirers what you are looking for and what you have to offer.

"If you're not branding yourself,
you can be sure others will do it for you!"

"If you're not branding yourself,
you can be sure others will do it for you!"

"If you're not branding yourself,
you can be sure others will do it for you!"

_____

_____

_____

_____

_____

_____

_____

_____

_____

_____

_____

_____

_____

_____

_____

_____

_____

_____

_____

_____

_____

_____

_____

"If you're not branding yourself,
you can be sure others will do it for you!"

"If you're not branding yourself,
you can be sure others will do it for you!"

"If you're not branding yourself,
you can be sure others will do it for you!"

_____

_____

_____

_____

_____

_____

_____

_____

_____

_____

_____

_____

_____

_____

_____

_____

_____

_____

_____

_____

_____

_____

"If you're not branding yourself,
you can be sure others will do it for you!"

"If you're not branding yourself,
you can be sure others will do it for you!"

"If you're not branding yourself,
you can be sure others will do it for you!"

YOUR CV

Your main tool to initially demonstrate to employers that you are a credible candidate is your CV. Invest time in it and make sure it is customised for every role you apply for.

A startling fact is that when your CV lands in a recruiter's inbox you only have a few seconds to make an impact and land in the yes or maybe pile for further consideration. Some roles attract hundreds of applications so it is vital that your front page stands out in the right way. Recruiters rely on the important facts being easy to see in a concisely presented resume, to help you get invited to a meeting follow these points:

FIRSTLY

Stand back to review your CV; what do you want your CV to say?

Ask others what your CV says to them; is it conveying the right message?

There are many views and opinions on the best way to write your CV and it is worth considering hiring the services of a professional CV writer to help you.

Some top tips for writing your CV yourself.

- The optimal CV length is 3 pages for someone with an established career, however page one Is the critical one to get right.

- Never just update an old CV with your current job, keep your CV relevant (see section 7 of this journal).

- Make sure that you have your full contact details and location at the top of the CV, a link to your LinkedIn profile, and that your contact details such as email address are appropriate for a professional application!

- Exclude personal information such as your date of birth and a photograph as well as removing any old irrelevant information.

- Beware of writing a profile which has questionable phrases such as 'hard-working', 'highly motivated' or 'team-player'. None of these are qualified by the information in your CV, so if you include a profile, use action words which describe your skills and experience such as created, transformed, influenced, organised.

- Always review the CV you are submitting to a company against the requirements of the role. To reflect the different type of roles you may apply for, I recommend that you have more than one version of your CV, (keep a note in the tracker of which version you have sent). Always use the Reality Check exercise to sense - check your application.

- Make sure it is accurate – dates, job titles and qualifications.

- With an established career you should summarise your work history on page one along with key achievements expressed in facts, making the CV immediately easy to read and relevant for the recruiter.

- Include relevant roles outside of work - voluntary positions, work placements, temporary posts, if they add value to your application.

- Use a readable professional text such as Helvetica (recognised as having excellent clarity for reading quickly and easily. Alternatively, Garamond, Calibri, or Gils Sans are all recognised as good CV fonts.

- Above all keep it concise and impactful!

EVALUATION & FEEDBACK

If you have interviewed for a role internally or through a recruitment agency you should hopefully receive feedback. Always call your recruitment consultant after your interview to share feedback. Quality of their feedback will vary with recruitment consultants, often because their client has not been forthcoming or because they have been over-whelmed by the volume of applicants, but always request it! It is unusual to receive detailed feedback from a direct application to a company.

In addition to requesting feedback, you should stand back and objectively give yourself feedback immediately after an interview on your performance.

Use the following model to honestly assess your performance and record your notes in your tracker.

SMART INTERVIEWING:

- What was the question asked?
- What was your answer?
- Did it make the right impact?
- How could you have improved on the answer?

If you are required to prepare a presentation or take a psychometric test, reflect afterwards about how you found the process and what additional preparation would have added value. Plus, ask if it's possible to have a copy of any testing before or after you take them, as often the same tests are requested for similar roles, and it will help you to be prepared.

Learn from every single meeting, don't get despondent by the rejections, put on your 'Project YOU' persona, evaluate and work on improving next time, e.g., think how to just 'tweak an answer' so it lands more effectively. Plus, if it went well acknowledge what worked and keep it in your mental toolkit.

It is important to keep in mind that employers always have a choice of at least two or three people who meet a role brief and it can be the smallest differential that decides the outcome. So keep practising, researching, networking and reviewing and don't be despondent because it shows!

IS THIS THE ROLE FOR ME –
am I the right person for this role?

I always visualise a seesaw when discussing if a candidate is making the right choice in accepting a role and if the client is making the right offer! As long as the seesaw is level and both parties are gaining equally, the seesaw will stay flat and no one will fall off. Think back if that has always been the case for your career? What are your realisations?

Consider:

- Why did I accept the role?

- What was the mismatch?

- Was I properly inducted and trained?

- Do I feel I took the role for the wrong reasons?

- What have I learnt that I need to know more about before applying & accepting a future role?

MANAGING OFFERS

You have an offer! Congratulations!

If you have followed the process in the journal, especially the deep dive evaluation of why the role is 'right for you', then the offer should be a close fit to your aspirations.

Now forget the euphoria (for an hour or so!), and take time to look at some key points:

· What doubts, if any, do you have and what will help you overcome with these?

· Do you have a clear picture of how your role fits into the business structure and what is expected of you?

· Have you established how your success will be measured? Are you clear on the expectations and timelines? Do you know what's ahead?

· Does the job add value to your CV and long-term plans?

· Are there any logistical challenges? For example the journey or working from home?

· Are there elements of the offer that you want to negotiate? (Check when the next pay review is due, it may be more than a year away depending on your joining date). Now is the time to negotiate as much as possible, it's much harder once you are inside the organisation.

· Have you met the team? Perhaps you've had an informal coffee meeting or gained a sense of the working environment and team values?

· Talk with someone you trust and value the opinion of in the workplace about the offer, and consider the pro's and con's before making your final decision to accept or decline the job.

QUESTIONS TO ASK ABOUT THE OFFER

Writing down your thoughts and the facts is proven to give you clarity and commitment. So use the next couple of pages to write down how you feel about the offer and the closeness of the fit to what you want. This will help you to get very clear on why this is, or isn't, the right role for you, putting this information at the forefront of your mind when you are making your decision.

'PROJECT YOU'
TAKING ACTION

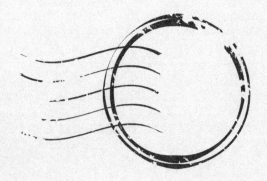

The distance
between your
dreams and reality
is called ACTION

UNKNOWN

PROJECT YOU:
Using the application tracker

So, accept that you may start this journey and make some wrong moves along the way, rocky days and disappointments. But being pro-active and learning is positive action, it's better than staying stuck in a miserable situation due to doing nothing. Take action 'mindfully' and keep your goals front of mind at times during 'Project YOU'!

This section of the journal is the one you should use for every single role you consider applying for, not just the ones you do actually go on to apply for. There are 4 pages for every role; the first two pages are where you validate for yourself if this role is right for you to progress to an application. Use the My Notes page to record what you have researched about the business. This could include exploring if you have any connections or know anyone in a similar role that you can speak with to find out more about the job or company. Never underestimate the value of research and networking in planning your application.

These 4 tracking pages are also available in Google Docs, please send an email to **hello@elevatecareerscoach.com** with a copy of your journal receipt to request your copy of the digital templates.

Take time to decide what version of your CV is most relevant to the role you are applying for. Craft a cover letter and use the form to record everything that you know about the role and application process. This means that when the recruiter calls you can use your journal as a prompt, enabling you to talk confidently about your application and answer all their questions. Remember almost 50% of calls recruiters and hiring managers make are met with candidates unable to recall the role or the details - this alone will give you a head start in standing out as a great potential candidate.

MY RESEARCH NOTES AND FACTS

"Opportunities don't happen, you create them"

REALITY CHECKER

JOB TITLE APPLIED FOR:

COMPANY:

DATE OF ADVERT:

TARGET: Minimum 50% match, ideal 70% match

KNOWLEDGE & SKILLS SOUGHT	MY SKILLS	EXPERIENCE SOUGHT	MY EXPERIENCE
TOTALS: What is your % match?			

TRACKING YOUR PROGRESS

COMPANY	ROLE/TITLE	ADVERTISED SALARY	SOURCE	DATE APPLIED

MY NETWORK/LINKEDIN CONNECTIONS

CV USED	CONTACT NAME	RESPONSE	INTERVIEW DATE	OUTCOME

MY SKILLS/STRENGTHS

MY RESEARCH NOTES AND FACTS

"Opportunities don't happen,
you create them"

REALITY CHECKER

JOB TITLE APPLIED FOR:

COMPANY:

DATE OF ADVERT:

TARGET: Minimum 50% match, ideal 70% match

KNOWLEDGE & SKILLS SOUGHT	MY SKILLS	EXPERIENCE SOUGHT	MY EXPERIENCE
TOTALS: What is your % match?			

TRACKING YOUR PROGRESS

COMPANY	ROLE/TITLE	ADVERTISED SALARY	SOURCE	DATE APPLIED

MY NETWORK/LINKEDIN CONNECTIONS

CV USED	CONTACT NAME	RESPONSE	INTERVIEW DATE	OUTCOME

MY SKILLS/STRENGTHS

MY RESEARCH NOTES AND FACTS

"Opportunities don't happen, you create them"

REALITY CHECKER

JOB TITLE APPLIED FOR:

COMPANY:

DATE OF ADVERT:

TARGET: Minimum 50% match, ideal 70% match

KNOWLEDGE & SKILLS SOUGHT	MY SKILLS	EXPERIENCE SOUGHT	MY EXPERIENCE
TOTALS: What is your % match?			

TRACKING YOUR PROGRESS

COMPANY	ROLE/TITLE	ADVERTISED SALARY	SOURCE	DATE APPLIED

MY NETWORK/LINKEDIN CONNECTIONS

CV USED	CONTACT NAME	RESPONSE	INTERVIEW DATE	OUTCOME

MY SKILLS/STRENGTHS

MY RESEARCH NOTES
AND FACTS

"Opportunities don't happen,
you create them"

REALITY CHECKER

JOB TITLE APPLIED FOR:

COMPANY:

DATE OF ADVERT:

TARGET: Minimum 50% match, ideal 70% match

KNOWLEDGE & SKILLS SOUGHT	MY SKILLS	EXPERIENCE SOUGHT	MY EXPERIENCE
TOTALS: What is your % match?			

TRACKING YOUR PROGRESS

COMPANY	ROLE/TITLE	ADVERTISED SALARY	SOURCE	DATE APPLIED

MY NETWORK/LINKEDIN CONNECTIONS

CV USED	CONTACT NAME	RESPONSE	INTERVIEW DATE	OUTCOME

MY SKILLS/STRENGTHS

MY RESEARCH NOTES AND FACTS

"Opportunities don't happen, you create them"

_____

_____

_____

_____

_____

_____

_____

_____

_____

_____

_____

_____

_____

_____

_____

_____

_____

_____

_____

_____

_____

_____

_____

REALITY CHECKER

JOB TITLE APPLIED FOR:

COMPANY:

DATE OF ADVERT:

TARGET: Minimum 50% match, ideal 70% match

KNOWLEDGE & SKILLS SOUGHT	MY SKILLS	EXPERIENCE SOUGHT	MY EXPERIENCE
TOTALS: What is your % match?			

TRACKING YOUR PROGRESS

COMPANY	ROLE/TITLE	ADVERTISED SALARY	SOURCE	DATE APPLIED

MY NETWORK/LINKEDIN CONNECTIONS

CV USED	CONTACT NAME	RESPONSE	INTERVIEW DATE	OUTCOME

MY SKILLS/STRENGTHS

MY RESEARCH NOTES AND FACTS

"Opportunities don't happen, you create them"

REALITY CHECKER

JOB TITLE APPLIED FOR:

COMPANY:

DATE OF ADVERT:

TARGET: Minimum 50% match, ideal 70% match

KNOWLEDGE & SKILLS SOUGHT	MY SKILLS	EXPERIENCE SOUGHT	MY EXPERIENCE
TOTALS: What is your % match?			

TRACKING YOUR PROGRESS

COMPANY	ROLE/TITLE	ADVERTISED SALARY	SOURCE	DATE APPLIED

MY NETWORK/LINKEDIN CONNECTIONS

CV USED	CONTACT NAME	RESPONSE	INTERVIEW DATE	OUTCOME

MY SKILLS/STRENGTHS

MY RESEARCH NOTES AND FACTS

"Opportunities don't happen,
you create them"

REALITY CHECKER

JOB TITLE APPLIED FOR:

COMPANY:

DATE OF ADVERT:

TARGET: Minimum 50% match, ideal 70% match

KNOWLEDGE & SKILLS SOUGHT	MY SKILLS	EXPERIENCE SOUGHT	MY EXPERIENCE
TOTALS: What is your % match?			

TRACKING YOUR PROGRESS

COMPANY	ROLE/TITLE	ADVERTISED SALARY	SOURCE	DATE APPLIED

MY NETWORK/LINKEDIN CONNECTIONS

CV USED	CONTACT NAME	RESPONSE	INTERVIEW DATE	OUTCOME

MY SKILLS/STRENGTHS

MY RESEARCH NOTES
AND FACTS

"Opportunities don't happen, you create them"

_____

_____

_____

_____

_____

_____

_____

_____

_____

_____

_____

_____

_____

_____

_____

_____

_____

_____

_____

_____

_____

_____

_____

REALITY CHECKER

JOB TITLE APPLIED FOR:

COMPANY:

DATE OF ADVERT:

TARGET: Minimum 50% match, ideal 70% match

KNOWLEDGE & SKILLS SOUGHT	MY SKILLS	EXPERIENCE SOUGHT	MY EXPERIENCE
TOTALS: What is your % match?			

TRACKING YOUR PROGRESS

COMPANY	ROLE/TITLE	ADVERTISED SALARY	SOURCE	DATE APPLIED

MY NETWORK/LINKEDIN CONNECTIONS

CV USED	CONTACT NAME	RESPONSE	INTERVIEW DATE	OUTCOME

MY SKILLS/STRENGTHS

MY RESEARCH NOTES AND FACTS

"Opportunities don't happen, you create them"

REALITY CHECKER

JOB TITLE APPLIED FOR:

COMPANY:

DATE OF ADVERT:

TARGET: Minimum 50% match, ideal 70% match

KNOWLEDGE & SKILLS SOUGHT	MY SKILLS	EXPERIENCE SOUGHT	MY EXPERIENCE
TOTALS: What is your % match?			

TRACKING YOUR PROGRESS

COMPANY	ROLE/TITLE	ADVERTISED SALARY	SOURCE	DATE APPLIED

MY NETWORK/LINKEDIN CONNECTIONS

CV USED	CONTACT NAME	RESPONSE	INTERVIEW DATE	OUTCOME

MY SKILLS/STRENGTHS

MY RESEARCH NOTES AND FACTS

"Opportunities don't happen,
you create them"

_____

_____

_____

_____

_____

_____

_____

_____

_____

_____

_____

_____

_____

_____

_____

_____

_____

_____

_____

_____

_____

_____

_____

REALITY CHECKER

JOB TITLE APPLIED FOR:

COMPANY:

DATE OF ADVERT:

TARGET: Minimum 50% match, ideal 70% match

KNOWLEDGE & SKILLS SOUGHT	MY SKILLS	EXPERIENCE SOUGHT	MY EXPERIENCE
TOTALS: What is your % match?			

TRACKING YOUR PROGRESS

COMPANY	ROLE/TITLE	ADVERTISED SALARY	SOURCE	DATE APPLIED

MY NETWORK/LINKEDIN CONNECTIONS

CV USED	CONTACT NAME	RESPONSE	INTERVIEW DATE	OUTCOME

MY SKILLS/STRENGTHS

MY RESEARCH NOTES AND FACTS

"Opportunities don't happen,
you create them"

REALITY CHECKER

JOB TITLE APPLIED FOR:

COMPANY:

DATE OF ADVERT:

TARGET: Minimum 50% match, ideal 70% match

KNOWLEDGE & SKILLS SOUGHT	MY SKILLS	EXPERIENCE SOUGHT	MY EXPERIENCE
TOTALS: What is your % match?			

TRACKING YOUR PROGRESS

COMPANY	ROLE/TITLE	ADVERTISED SALARY	SOURCE	DATE APPLIED

MY NETWORK/LINKEDIN CONNECTIONS

CV USED	CONTACT NAME	RESPONSE	INTERVIEW DATE	OUTCOME

MY SKILLS/STRENGTHS

MY RESEARCH NOTES AND FACTS

"Opportunities don't happen, you create them"

REALITY CHECKER

JOB TITLE APPLIED FOR:

COMPANY:

DATE OF ADVERT:

TARGET: Minimum 50% match, ideal 70% match

KNOWLEDGE & SKILLS SOUGHT	MY SKILLS	EXPERIENCE SOUGHT	MY EXPERIENCE
TOTALS: What is your % match?			

TRACKING YOUR PROGRESS

COMPANY	ROLE/TITLE	ADVERTISED SALARY	SOURCE	DATE APPLIED

MY NETWORK/LINKEDIN CONNECTIONS

CV USED	CONTACT NAME	RESPONSE	INTERVIEW DATE	OUTCOME

MY SKILLS/STRENGTHS

MY RESEARCH NOTES AND FACTS

"Opportunities don't happen, you create them"

REALITY CHECKER

JOB TITLE APPLIED FOR:

COMPANY:

DATE OF ADVERT:

TARGET: Minimum 50% match, ideal 70% match

KNOWLEDGE & SKILLS SOUGHT	MY SKILLS	EXPERIENCE SOUGHT	MY EXPERIENCE
TOTALS: What is your % match?			

TRACKING YOUR PROGRESS

COMPANY	ROLE/TITLE	ADVERTISED SALARY	SOURCE	DATE APPLIED

MY NETWORK/LINKEDIN CONNECTIONS

CV USED	CONTACT NAME	RESPONSE	INTERVIEW DATE	OUTCOME

MY SKILLS/STRENGTHS

MY RESEARCH NOTES AND FACTS

"Opportunities don't happen,
you create them"

_____

_____

_____

_____

_____

_____

_____

_____

_____

_____

_____

_____

_____

_____

_____

_____

_____

_____

_____

_____

_____

_____

_____

_____

REALITY CHECKER

JOB TITLE APPLIED FOR:

COMPANY:

DATE OF ADVERT:

TARGET: Minimum 50% match, ideal 70% match

KNOWLEDGE & SKILLS SOUGHT	MY SKILLS	EXPERIENCE SOUGHT	MY EXPERIENCE
TOTALS: What is your % match?			

TRACKING YOUR PROGRESS

COMPANY	ROLE/TITLE	ADVERTISED SALARY	SOURCE	DATE APPLIED

MY NETWORK/LINKEDIN CONNECTIONS

CV USED	CONTACT NAME	RESPONSE	INTERVIEW DATE	OUTCOME

MY SKILLS/STRENGTHS

MY RESEARCH NOTES AND FACTS

"Opportunities don't happen, you create them"

REALITY CHECKER

JOB TITLE APPLIED FOR:

COMPANY:

DATE OF ADVERT:

TARGET: Minimum 50% match, ideal 70% match

KNOWLEDGE & SKILLS SOUGHT	MY SKILLS	EXPERIENCE SOUGHT	MY EXPERIENCE
TOTALS: What is your % match?			

TRACKING YOUR PROGRESS

COMPANY	ROLE/TITLE	ADVERTISED SALARY	SOURCE	DATE APPLIED

MY NETWORK/LINKEDIN CONNECTIONS

CV USED	CONTACT NAME	RESPONSE	INTERVIEW DATE	OUTCOME

MY SKILLS/STRENGTHS

MY RESEARCH NOTES AND FACTS

"Opportunities don't happen, you create them"

REALITY CHECKER

JOB TITLE APPLIED FOR:

COMPANY:

DATE OF ADVERT:

TARGET: Minimum 50% match, ideal 70% match

KNOWLEDGE & SKILLS SOUGHT	MY SKILLS	EXPERIENCE SOUGHT	MY EXPERIENCE
TOTALS: What is your % match?			

TRACKING YOUR PROGRESS

COMPANY	ROLE/TITLE	ADVERTISED SALARY	SOURCE	DATE APPLIED

MY NETWORK/LINKEDIN CONNECTIONS

CV USED	CONTACT NAME	RESPONSE	INTERVIEW DATE	OUTCOME

MY SKILLS/STRENGTHS

MY RESEARCH NOTES AND FACTS

"Opportunities don't happen, you create them"

_____

_____

_____

_____

_____

_____

_____

_____

_____

_____

_____

_____

_____

_____

_____

_____

_____

_____

_____

_____

_____

_____

_____

_____

_____

_____

REALITY CHECKER

JOB TITLE APPLIED FOR:

COMPANY:

DATE OF ADVERT:

TARGET: Minimum 50% match, ideal 70% match

KNOWLEDGE & SKILLS SOUGHT	MY SKILLS	EXPERIENCE SOUGHT	MY EXPERIENCE
TOTALS: What is your % match?			

TRACKING YOUR PROGRESS

COMPANY	ROLE/TITLE	ADVERTISED SALARY	SOURCE	DATE APPLIED

MY NETWORK/LINKEDIN CONNECTIONS

CV USED	CONTACT NAME	RESPONSE	INTERVIEW DATE	OUTCOME

MY SKILLS/STRENGTHS

MY RESEARCH NOTES AND FACTS

"Opportunities don't happen, you create them"

REALITY CHECKER

JOB TITLE APPLIED FOR:

COMPANY:

DATE OF ADVERT:

TARGET: Minimum 50% match, ideal 70% match

KNOWLEDGE & SKILLS SOUGHT	MY SKILLS	EXPERIENCE SOUGHT	MY EXPERIENCE
TOTALS: What is your % match?			

TRACKING YOUR PROGRESS

COMPANY	ROLE/TITLE	ADVERTISED SALARY	SOURCE	DATE APPLIED

MY NETWORK/LINKEDIN CONNECTIONS

CV USED	CONTACT NAME	RESPONSE	INTERVIEW DATE	OUTCOME

MY SKILLS/STRENGTHS

MY RESEARCH NOTES AND FACTS

"Opportunities don't happen, you create them"

REALITY CHECKER

JOB TITLE APPLIED FOR:

COMPANY:

DATE OF ADVERT:

TARGET: Minimum 50% match, ideal 70% match

KNOWLEDGE & SKILLS SOUGHT	MY SKILLS	EXPERIENCE SOUGHT	MY EXPERIENCE
TOTALS: What is your % match?			

TRACKING YOUR PROGRESS

COMPANY	ROLE/TITLE	ADVERTISED SALARY	SOURCE	DATE APPLIED

MY NETWORK/LINKEDIN CONNECTIONS

CV USED	CONTACT NAME	RESPONSE	INTERVIEW DATE	OUTCOME

MY SKILLS/STRENGTHS

MY RESEARCH NOTES
AND FACTS

"Opportunities don't happen, you create them"

_____

_____

_____

_____

_____

_____

_____

_____

_____

_____

_____

_____

_____

_____

_____

_____

_____

_____

_____

_____

_____

_____

REALITY CHECKER

JOB TITLE APPLIED FOR:

COMPANY:

DATE OF ADVERT:

TARGET: Minimum 50% match, ideal 70% match

KNOWLEDGE & SKILLS SOUGHT	MY SKILLS	EXPERIENCE SOUGHT	MY EXPERIENCE
TOTALS: What is your % match?			

TRACKING YOUR PROGRESS

COMPANY	ROLE/TITLE	ADVERTISED SALARY	SOURCE	DATE APPLIED

MY NETWORK/LINKEDIN CONNECTIONS

CV USED	CONTACT NAME	RESPONSE	INTERVIEW DATE	OUTCOME

MY SKILLS/STRENGTHS

MY RESEARCH NOTES AND FACTS

"Opportunities don't happen, you create them"

REALITY CHECKER

JOB TITLE APPLIED FOR:

COMPANY:

DATE OF ADVERT:

TARGET: Minimum 50% match, ideal 70% match

KNOWLEDGE & SKILLS SOUGHT	MY SKILLS	EXPERIENCE SOUGHT	MY EXPERIENCE
TOTALS: What is your % match?			

TRACKING YOUR PROGRESS

COMPANY	ROLE/TITLE	ADVERTISED SALARY	SOURCE	DATE APPLIED

MY NETWORK/LINKEDIN CONNECTIONS

CV USED	CONTACT NAME	RESPONSE	INTERVIEW DATE	OUTCOME

MY SKILLS/STRENGTHS

MY RESEARCH NOTES AND FACTS

"Opportunities don't happen, you create them"

REALITY CHECKER

JOB TITLE APPLIED FOR:

COMPANY:

DATE OF ADVERT:

TARGET: Minimum 50% match, ideal 70% match

KNOWLEDGE & SKILLS SOUGHT	MY SKILLS	EXPERIENCE SOUGHT	MY EXPERIENCE
TOTALS: What is your % match?			

TRACKING YOUR PROGRESS

COMPANY	ROLE/TITLE	ADVERTISED SALARY	SOURCE	DATE APPLIED

MY NETWORK/LINKEDIN CONNECTIONS

CV USED	CONTACT NAME	RESPONSE	INTERVIEW DATE	OUTCOME

MY SKILLS/STRENGTHS

MY RESEARCH NOTES AND FACTS

"Opportunities don't happen, you create them"

REALITY CHECKER

JOB TITLE APPLIED FOR:

COMPANY:

DATE OF ADVERT:

TARGET: Minimum 50% match, ideal 70% match

KNOWLEDGE & SKILLS SOUGHT	MY SKILLS	EXPERIENCE SOUGHT	MY EXPERIENCE
TOTALS: What is your % match?			

TRACKING YOUR PROGRESS

COMPANY	ROLE/TITLE	ADVERTISED SALARY	SOURCE	DATE APPLIED

MY NETWORK/LINKEDIN CONNECTIONS

CV USED	CONTACT NAME	RESPONSE	INTERVIEW DATE	OUTCOME

MY SKILLS/STRENGTHS

MY RESEARCH NOTES AND FACTS

"Opportunities don't happen, you create them"

REALITY CHECKER

JOB TITLE APPLIED FOR:

COMPANY:

DATE OF ADVERT:

TARGET: Minimum 50% match, ideal 70% match

KNOWLEDGE & SKILLS SOUGHT	MY SKILLS	EXPERIENCE SOUGHT	MY EXPERIENCE
TOTALS: What is your % match?			

TRACKING YOUR PROGRESS

COMPANY	ROLE/TITLE	ADVERTISED SALARY	SOURCE	DATE APPLIED

MY NETWORK/LINKEDIN CONNECTIONS

CV USED	CONTACT NAME	RESPONSE	INTERVIEW DATE	OUTCOME

MY SKILLS/STRENGTHS

MY RESEARCH NOTES AND FACTS

"Opportunities don't happen, you create them"

REALITY CHECKER

JOB TITLE APPLIED FOR:

COMPANY:

DATE OF ADVERT:

TARGET: Minimum 50% match, ideal 70% match

KNOWLEDGE & SKILLS SOUGHT	MY SKILLS	EXPERIENCE SOUGHT	MY EXPERIENCE
TOTALS: What is your % match?			

TRACKING YOUR PROGRESS

COMPANY	ROLE/TITLE	ADVERTISED SALARY	SOURCE	DATE APPLIED

MY NETWORK/LINKEDIN CONNECTIONS

CV USED	CONTACT NAME	RESPONSE	INTERVIEW DATE	OUTCOME

MY SKILLS/STRENGTHS

MY RESEARCH NOTES AND FACTS

"Opportunities don't happen, you create them"

_____

_____

_____

_____

_____

_____

_____

_____

_____

_____

_____

_____

_____

_____

_____

_____

_____

_____

_____

_____

_____

_____

REALITY CHECKER

JOB TITLE APPLIED FOR:

COMPANY:

DATE OF ADVERT:

TARGET: Minimum 50% match, ideal 70% match

KNOWLEDGE & SKILLS SOUGHT	MY SKILLS	EXPERIENCE SOUGHT	MY EXPERIENCE
TOTALS: What is your % match?			

TRACKING YOUR PROGRESS

COMPANY	ROLE/TITLE	ADVERTISED SALARY	SOURCE	DATE APPLIED

MY NETWORK/LINKEDIN CONNECTIONS

CV USED	CONTACT NAME	RESPONSE	INTERVIEW DATE	OUTCOME

MY SKILLS/STRENGTHS

MY RESEARCH NOTES AND FACTS

"Opportunities don't happen, you create them"

REALITY CHECKER

JOB TITLE APPLIED FOR:

COMPANY:

DATE OF ADVERT:

TARGET: Minimum 50% match, ideal 70% match

KNOWLEDGE & SKILLS SOUGHT	MY SKILLS	EXPERIENCE SOUGHT	MY EXPERIENCE
TOTALS: What is your % match?			

TRACKING YOUR PROGRESS

COMPANY	ROLE/TITLE	ADVERTISED SALARY	SOURCE	DATE APPLIED

MY NETWORK/LINKEDIN CONNECTIONS

CV USED	CONTACT NAME	RESPONSE	INTERVIEW DATE	OUTCOME

MY SKILLS/STRENGTHS

MY RESEARCH NOTES AND FACTS

"Opportunities don't happen, you create them"

REALITY CHECKER

JOB TITLE APPLIED FOR:

COMPANY:

DATE OF ADVERT:

TARGET: Minimum 50% match, ideal 70% match

KNOWLEDGE & SKILLS SOUGHT	MY SKILLS	EXPERIENCE SOUGHT	MY EXPERIENCE
TOTALS: What is your % match?			

TRACKING YOUR PROGRESS

COMPANY	ROLE/TITLE	ADVERTISED SALARY	SOURCE	DATE APPLIED

MY NETWORK/LINKEDIN CONNECTIONS

CV USED	CONTACT NAME	RESPONSE	INTERVIEW DATE	OUTCOME

MY SKILLS/STRENGTHS

MY RESEARCH NOTES AND FACTS

"Opportunities don't happen, you create them"

REALITY CHECKER

JOB TITLE APPLIED FOR:

COMPANY:

DATE OF ADVERT:

TARGET: Minimum 50% match, ideal 70% match

KNOWLEDGE & SKILLS SOUGHT	MY SKILLS	EXPERIENCE SOUGHT	MY EXPERIENCE
TOTALS: What is your % match?			

TRACKING YOUR PROGRESS

COMPANY	ROLE/TITLE	ADVERTISED SALARY	SOURCE	DATE APPLIED

MY NETWORK/LINKEDIN CONNECTIONS

CV USED	CONTACT NAME	RESPONSE	INTERVIEW DATE	OUTCOME

MY SKILLS/STRENGTHS

MY RESEARCH NOTES AND FACTS

"Opportunities don't happen, you create them"

REALITY CHECKER

JOB TITLE APPLIED FOR:

COMPANY:

DATE OF ADVERT:

TARGET: Minimum 50% match, ideal 70% match

KNOWLEDGE & SKILLS SOUGHT	MY SKILLS	EXPERIENCE SOUGHT	MY EXPERIENCE
TOTALS: What is your % match?			

TRACKING YOUR PROGRESS

COMPANY	ROLE/TITLE	ADVERTISED SALARY	SOURCE	DATE APPLIED

MY NETWORK/LINKEDIN CONNECTIONS

CV USED	CONTACT NAME	RESPONSE	INTERVIEW DATE	OUTCOME

MY SKILLS/STRENGTHS

YOUR CAREER REFLECTIONS

This section is to track and support your development and learning in the first 90 days of your new job or promotion. By completing it you will give yourself time to reflect on your new role; what is going well, what has been unexpected and how you would like to see your progression. These are all topics your Line Manager may discuss with you at performance reviews, so being prepared is vital.

Moving forward, after your first 90 days, there is great value in spending designated time each week, or even month, reflecting on what has gone well, or not. As well as how you have managed situations and the outcomes. This provides you a private moment with yourself in which to be honest about topics such as the project outcomes and relationship building. You can ask yourself questions such as; what have I learnt about myself? What could I have done better? What have I most enjoyed?

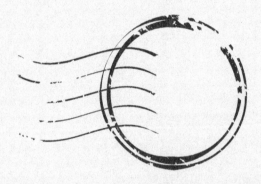

Gibbs model of reflections gives structure to this process▫

The aim of this as a regular ongoing activity, even when you are settled in a great job, is to make you stop and think about your own performance and the ways in which you can improve or ask for support. In addition to this, it will also jog your memory when you meet with your coach or mentor, update your CV or prepare for a performance review.

This can be a brilliant tool to support you in preparation for an interview as you'll be looking for examples to evidence how you have managed both positive and challenging situations.

DESCRIPTION
What is your
current situation?

FEELINGS
What are you
thinking and
feeling?

ACTION
What steps do
you need to take?

Career
reflections

EVALUATION
What is working/
not working?

CONCLUSION
What are your
options?

ANALYSIS
How is this part of
the big picture?

Based on Gibbs Model of Reflection

The following pages should be used to develop the habit of regular reflection as these are useful notes and reminders for you to form ideas and gather facts and topics for your performance review meetings, or discussions with your coach.

Date

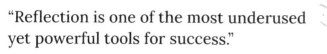

"Reflection is one of the most underused yet powerful tools for success."

RICHARD CARLSON

Date

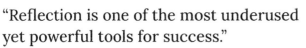

"Reflection is one of the most underused yet powerful tools for success."

RICHARD CARLSON

Date

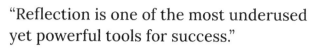

"Reflection is one of the most underused yet powerful tools for success."

RICHARD CARLSON

Date

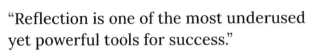

"Reflection is one of the most underused yet powerful tools for success."

RICHARD CARLSON

Date

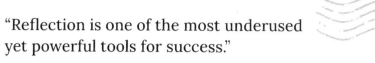

"Reflection is one of the most underused yet powerful tools for success."

RICHARD CARLSON

Date

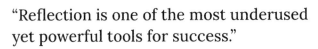

"Reflection is one of the most underused yet powerful tools for success."

RICHARD CARLSON

Date

"Reflection is one of the most underused yet powerful tools for success."

RICHARD CARLSON

Date

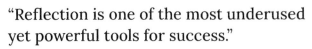

"Reflection is one of the most underused yet powerful tools for success."

RICHARD CARLSON

Date

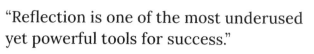

"Reflection is one of the most underused yet powerful tools for success."

RICHARD CARLSON

Date

KEEPING TRACK

As your career develops and you change job role or organisation much of the detail can 'blur' so maintaining an accurate CV and salary details becomes a challenge. By keep quick simple records updating your CV or providing reference information becomes easier.

Things to record include dates and facts such as reporting structures, size of remit, budget accountability, team size - and your salary/package info.

Date

Don't get side-tracked from keeping track!

Date

Don't get side-tracked from keeping track!

Date

Don't get side-tracked from keeping track!

Date

Don't get side-tracked from keeping track!

Date

Don't get side-tracked from keeping track!

Date

Don't get side-tracked from keeping track!

Date

Don't get side-tracked from keeping track!

Date

Don't get side-tracked from keeping track!

Date

Don't get side-tracked from keeping track!

Date

IN SUMMARY

The current job market is very changeable with the impact of the global pandemic, baby boomers now retiring, and a whole new way of working from home... let alone the challenges of the global economy! Taking into account the impact of all of these factors, even if you are in a job you enjoy but want to get ahead, it is important to arm yourself with the best qualifications and strategy to support you in moving towards achieving your next career change or move.

I look forward to hearing from you about how you have used this journal and how it has supported your career change or job search journey.

Please do get in touch **https://linktr.ee/elevatecareercoach**

Elevate
CAREER COACH

SINCE 1991.

Printed in Great Britain
by Amazon